101 Things I Learned in Business School

101 Things I Learned™ in Business School

Michael W. Preis with Matthew Frederick

illustrations by Matthew Frederick

Matthew Frederick is the series creator, editor, and illustrator.

This publication is designed to provide competent and reliable information regarding the subject matter covered. However, it is sold with the understanding that the author and publisher are not engaged in rendering legal, financial, or other professional advice. Laws and practices often vary from state to state and if legal or other expert assistance is required, the services of a professional should be sought. The author and publisher specifically disclaim any liability that is incurred from the use or application of the contents of this book.

Grand Central Publishing
Hachette Book Group
237 Park Avenue
New York, NY 10017
www.HachetteBookGroup.com

Printed in China

First Edition: May 2010
10 9 8 7 6 5

Grand Central Publishing is a division of Hachette Book Group, Inc. The Grand Central Publishing name and logo is a trademark of Hachette Book Group, Inc.

The Hachette Speakers Bureau provides a wide range of authors for speaking events. To find out more, go to www.hachettespeakersbureau.com or call (866) 376-6591.

The publisher is not responsible for websites (or their content) that are not owned by the publisher.

Library of Congress Cataloging-in-Publication Data
Preis, Michael W.
  101 things I learned in business school / by Michael W. Preis, with Matthew Frederick.—1st ed.
      p. cm.
  ISBN 978-0-446-55028-4
  1. Management. 2. Finance. 3. Commerce. 4. Business—Study and teaching. I. Frederick, Matthew. II. Title.
III. Title: One hundred one things I learned in business school.
  HD31.P669 2010
  658—dc22
                                                                                                    2009037648

From Michael

To my mother, Elinor B. Preis, for always believing in me

Author's Note

An MBA is one of the most sought after postgraduate degrees, viewed by many as a reliable avenue to a good job and lucrative career. However, while an MBA can help jump-start one's career and may speed professional advancement, it isn't the most essential factor in a successful career.

As often happens, when the majority of people figure out the rules of the game, the game changes. The paradigm of spending an entire career with a single employer or within a single industry is far less common than it once was. Those starting their careers now are likely to work for multiple employers and even in multiple industries over the course of their working lives. Thus, being able to learn quickly, adapt to change, and employ ethical behavior, passion, and savvy thinking in the face of new challenges is crucial.

While business schools provide specific information, skills, and tools for tomorrow's business people, they more importantly should instill a desire and proficiency for learning beyond the classroom. Furthermore, there is no single discipline called *business*; it is, rather, a broad field of endeavor encompassing such diverse disciplines as accounting, communications, economics, finance, leadership, management, marketing, operations, psychology, sociology, and strategy. Those most likely to be successful in business in the long run have the broadest and most open understanding of it.

This book seeks to present lessons in the areas of business that are most likely to be useful to you, whether you are a student in the field, a longstanding businessperson, or someone with an interest in the field. It may be many years before you have the opportunity to apply some of the lessons, but it is my hope, nonetheless, that they will increase your understanding and help you navigate the interesting and challenging avenues of the business world.

Michael W. Preis

Acknowledgments

From Michael

Thanks to Sal Divita, Geoff Love, Kevin Waspi, Kevin Jackson, Joe Mahoney, Greg Kellar, Abbie Griffin, Bill Brooks.

From Matt

Thanks to Karen Andrews, Alissa Barron, David Blaisdell, Dick Canada, Paul Caulfield, Sorche Fairbank, Joel Garreau, Mary Helen Gillespie, Tracy Martin, Bill McKibben, Jim Monagle, Roni Noland, Camille O'Garro, Janet Reid, Kallie Shimek, Flag Tonuzi, Tom Whatley, Rick Wolff, and Luke Wroblewski.

101 Things I Learned in Business School

Seller

Material value
+ Profit
———————
= Selling price

Buyer

Material value
+ Emotional reward
———————
= Purchase price

Business is the exchange of entities to which values have been assigned.

In business transactions, the values assigned to goods, services, or money may be economic, emotional, or both. A business transaction works because each party assigns a higher value to what it receives than what it provides. A customer who buys a sweater for $50 values the sweater more than the $50; likewise, the seller values the $50 more than the sweater.

Value may be assigned on the basis of anticipated future value instead of current value. For example, one might "overpay" for an ice cream machine because of an expectation that it will generate future income. In this sense, business is sometimes defined as the exchange of current value for future value.

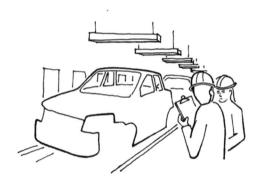

Business is not a single field of endeavor.

Accounting: the language of business, which organizes and conveys information about transactions in monetary terms

Finance: the management of money and monetary assets

Marketing: the effort to promote a company's products and brands to the intended markets, and to ensure that the right products are for sale at the right prices in the right places

Production and Operations: the coordination and overseeing of activities such as manufacturing and provision of services

Organizational Behavior: the study of how people act and interact in work settings; may include motivational strategies, corporate organization and culture, leadership models, group psychology, and conflict resolution

Economics: a social science pertaining to business and financial activity

Philosophy of business or business philosophy?

Business philosophy is a term used within the field of business to refer to the values or approach of a particular company (e.g., "ABC Widget's business philosophy is to put the customer first") or the dynamics of a market segment ("the widget industry demands a permanently flexible business philosophy").

The **philosophy of business** is concerned with broader meanings of business as a human endeavor, including whether business is fundamentally an economic or social phenomenon, the moral obligations of business to society, the degree to which government should regulate businesses, and the differences between business operations and meanings in capitalist and socialist societies.

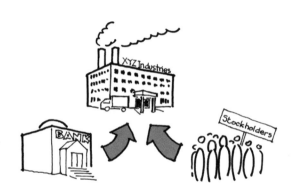

Capital is assets in the form of money or "near-money."

Equity capital is obtained by selling a portion of the ownership of a business to investors. It is considered *permanent capital* because the property or funding provided by the investors never has to be paid back. However, the investors—called equity owners or equity partners—may sell their ownership to other parties. Stocks are a form of equity ownership.

Debt capital is obtained by borrowing money. It is temporary in nature because the money must be repaid to the lenders. Bonds and bank loans are two sources of debt capital.

Not all capital is economic.

Intellectual capital is proprietary information and in-house knowledge of technologies, materials, processes, and markets useful to an organization.

Human capital consists of talents, skills, and knowledge residing among employees.

Social capital refers to established human relationships, both within and external to a company, that create and maintain value.

Brand equity is the additional value that a brand name adds to an otherwise equivalent good or service, allowing the company to charge a higher price.

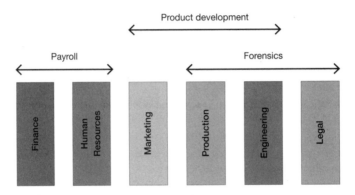

Many business activities have to be performed across functional silos.

6

Functional silos can be dysfunctional.

The many disciplines in business are often organized and studied independently. But while their separation can provide clarity and allow expertise to shine, "functional silos" are not inherently distinct. The actions of departments and their employees invariably affect other departments and the entire organization.

Business ownership

Sole proprietorship: The owner and the business are legally the same entity, although a separate business name may be used. It is the simplest form of ownership, and the owner is personally liable for all acts and debts of the company.

Partnership: The same as a sole proprietorship but with multiple owners. Partners' ownership interests need not be equal, but any partner may be liable for acts of the others. Liability is not proportional to ownership interest.

Corporation: An entity deemed legally distinct from its owners, who cannot be held personally liable for acts or debts of the corporation. The owners are stockholders, and the stock may be privately held (e.g., a family business) or publicly traded on a stock exchange. C corporations pay taxes based on net profit, while S corporations pass some income and losses to the owners for inclusion on their personal taxes.

Limited Liability Company: An unincorporated business that combines some of the simplicities and tax flexibility of sole proprietorships and partnerships with some of the liability advantages of a corporation.

A stock indicates ownership; a bond is an I.O.U.

8

Stocks are increments of ownership of a corporation. Bonds do not represent ownership, but are used by corporations and governments to borrow money.

Common stockholders elect a board of directors to oversee the company's management, and are usually paid a dividend if the company is profitable.

Preferred stockholders typically do not have voting rights but are given preference over common stockholders in the payment of dividends and liquidation. Some preferred stocks carry with them the right to be converted into common stock.

With **secured bonds**, the issuer pledges specific assets as collateral in exchange for cash. A mortgage bond is an example. In the event of bankruptcy, a court appointed trustee sells the assets and uses the proceeds to repay the bond holders.

Unsecured bonds, or debentures, are not backed by collateral. In the event of bankruptcy, bondholders compete with other creditors for repayment.

The board of directors

A corporation is required by law to have a board of directors, elected by and having a fiduciary responsibility to the owners (stockholders). A board should consist of experts in the industry and represent the long-term interests of the owners and other stakeholders.

A board governs at a strategic rather than day-to-day level. It establishes policy, sets direction, hires and supervises top management, is responsible for compliance with laws and regulations, and assures adequate resources for operations.

Directors of not-for-profit corporations do not represent stockholders, but the general public. Some boards—both non- and for-profit—consider themselves responsible to everyone with an interest in the corporation's activities, including customers, employees, suppliers, and the communities in which they operate.

How to run a meeting

- Create and distribute an agenda three to seven days in advance. Put the highest priority items at the top. Let the participants know ahead of time your expectations of them so they will be prepared.
- Depending on the formality of the meeting, consider designating someone to keep notes or minutes and watch the time.
- Begin on time. Review the agenda and ask if any changes are needed. Depending on the makeup and size of the group, the issues to be discussed, and other factors, you may need to set rules for behavior, e.g., only two minutes per person, everyone in the room must be heard from, etc.
- Follow the agenda and stay on subject. Encourage participation and debate by all, but other than scheduled break-out discussions, allow only one person to speak at a time.
- Draw clear conclusions, and vote on discussion items when appropriate.
- Outline the next actions to be taken by the group (things to do, next meeting, etc.). Provide a brief recap and reiterate assigned tasks.
- Shortly after the meeting, distribute notes or minutes, organized in a format similar to the agenda. Include the major discussion points and the conclusions reached, and solicit comments, questions, corrections, and clarifications.

Fastest Growing U.S. Industries, 2006–2016

Industry	Predicted growth
Management, scientific, and technical consulting services	78%
Services for the elderly and persons with disabilities	74%
Gambling industries	66%
Home health care services	55%
Educational support services	53%
Community care facilities, elderly	50%
Other financial investment activities	47%
Facilities support services	46%
Securities and commodity contracts, brokerages, and exchanges	46%
Internet publishing and broadcasting	44%

Source: U.S. Bureau of Labor Statistics

There are three ways to grow a business.

Increase market share. In a stagnant market (one with a constant overall size), a business can grow only by taking market share from competitors.

Grow with the market. If a market is growing, a business can expand by maintaining a constant market share.

Expand into a new market. In any market circumstance, but particularly in a stagnant market, a business may grow by expanding into a new (and usually related) market—for example, a dry cleaner that begins offering shoe repair or tuxedo rental.

Narrowly defined market

Broadly defined market

Don't just compete in existing markets; anticipate new ones.

Businesspeople sometimes restrict their vision of the future to a better, but vaguely defined, version of the present business. In doing so, they may miss opportunities for expansion into new and related industries. For example, a cable TV company that defines itself as providing television programming may be framing its future too narrowly. By redefining its mission as the transfer of information to and from homes, it positions itself to provide internet service, home security, home automation, and telephone service through the same cable.

"I skate to where the puck is going to be, not where it has been."

—Attributed to WAYNE GRETZKY

Malcolm Gladwell

Six degrees of Lois Weisberg

Personal connections are the best way to generate new business opportunities. But rather counterintuitively, the people to whom we are closest are often less likely to open new doors for us than those we barely know. This is because those we know well introduced us long ago to the opportunities they can provide, but those with whom we are barely familiar are connected to an entirely different network of opportunities.

Most localities have a few individuals who know a lot of people across social and professional boundaries and facilitate networking among them. The writer Malcolm Gladwell calls these people, such as Lois Weisberg in Chicago, *connectors*.

A mission or vision statement that is impossible to disagree with might not be saying much of significance.

15

A **mission statement** describes the current central purpose and goal of an organization, to guide daily decision making and performance. A **vision statement** describes what an organization seeks to become, or the ideal society to which the organization seeks to contribute.

When drafting and evaluating potential mission and vision statements, ask if the opposite of a proposed statement is obviously undesirable. If it is, the statement probably isn't saying anything particularly helpful. For example, a university mission statement that says the institution "seeks to produce highly effective, productive citizens" is unlikely to have any real influence on employees or students, since no university seeks to produce its opposite—ineffective, unproductive citizens. A more meaningful statement will assert that which is truly specific to the organization; it describes what the organization seeks to do that many or most of its peers do not.

16

Learn an organization's culture before working with or for it.

Organizational culture is the set of behaviors, norms, attitudes, priorities, and beliefs accepted by and within an organization. Cultures vary widely; in some, executives are aloof while in others they are more accessible. In some, processes and behaviors are ad hoc and quirky, while in others regimentation and predictability are norms. A poor cultural match not only can create discomfort for individual workers, but can compromise endeavors at a corporate scale—even undermining large mergers and partnerships that are a good match by other, noncultural measures.

17

The most difficult and time-consuming problems in business are not business problems.

Business endeavors are often complicated by human factors: misunderstand-ings, absenteeism, selfish agendas, ego clashes, personal business performed on company time, and more. The wise manager identifies and minimizes root factors in the work environment that contribute to people problems, works to resolve the problems that do occur, and conducts him- or herself as a model for others.

18

"If your thinking is sloppy, your business will be sloppy. If you are disorganized, your business will be disorganized. If you are greedy, your employees will be greedy, giving you less and less of themselves and always asking for more."

—MICHAEL GERBER

Magnitude
(size of reward)

Valence
(importance of reward)

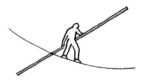

Expectancy
(likelihood of attainment)

Components of extrinsic motivation

Most employees want to do good work.

19

Workers may be motivated extrinsically or intrinsically. **Extrinsic motivation** derives from anticipation of external reaction, including praise, recognition, money (positive motivators), or punishment (negative motivator). Both positive and negative motivators have advantages and drawbacks: Positive motivators can lead workers to expect additional rewards for merely doing their jobs, while negative motivators may help get a task done but usually have a detrimental effect over the long run.

Intrinsic motivation comes from a worker's internal sense of purpose, personal enjoyment of the work, and satisfaction of a job done well. Intrinsic motivation can be furthered by employers by designing jobs to best suit employees, aggregating tasks in appealing ways, enlarging worker responsibilities, and increasing employee control over their own duties.

Top-Down
Example: U.S. auto industry

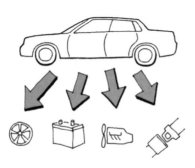

Manufacturers dictate
design and production
to suppliers.

Bottom-Up
Example: computer industry

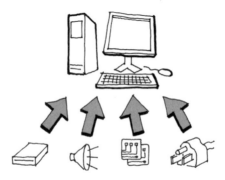

Inventors, manufacturers, and suppliers
create/provide components; other
manufacturers select and bundle them into
larger products.

Top-down and bottom-up

20

Top-down models of production and management are authority-based: The flow of information and processes originates in and is controlled by the upper tiers. They work best when a company's products and services are similar to those that were previously successful, when the upper tiers possess expertise or resources the lower tiers do not, and when the cost of mistakes by inexperienced staff would be prohibitive. Top-down models can be predictable and efficient, but also can become locked into outmoded habits.

In **bottom-up models**, information and processes originate in the lower tiers, usually in an open-ended, ad hoc manner. Bottom-up can work well in industries that are relatively new, in situations where the lower tiers possess unique expertise or resources, and when the cost of errors is not prohibitive. Bottom-up models often generate alternatives that top-down models cannot, but can also be chaotic and inefficient.

Command, consensus, or consultation?

Command decision making is the traditional top-down, hierarchical management model. It is most effective when processes or products are similar to previous examples and when management has knowledge and experience that lower-level staff does not. It is efficient but can be overreliant on old ways when a new approach is needed. Also, in a large, highly layered organization, command decisions by upper management may seem irrelevant to lower-level employees.

Consensus or democratic decisions are made by a majority of those most directly affected by the decision. Voices that might otherwise be unheard are allowed into the decision making process, but it can be inefficient, cacophonous, and confusing.

Consultative decision making hybridizes the preceding models. It is an authority-based model in which managers solicit input from the affected before making decisions. It is valued for allowing diverse voices into the process while yielding clear, final decisions for which one party is accountable.

A manager may use all three styles, switching from one to another depending on the situation.

Span of control

A manager usually should have no more than six to eight workers reporting to him or her.

When a small business expands, one frequently finds that a new layer of management is needed when it grows larger than six to eight people. Another layer is typically required at around thirty-six to sixty-four employees, and so on.

The ideal span of control depends on the nature of the work, the abilities of managers and workers, and the similarity or divergence of tasks being managed. Highly redundant processes such as manufacturing can have a very large span, while creative businesses such as architecture and filmmaking may have a span of only a few persons. But a good place to begin analyzing the span of control for most organizations is in the range of six to eight.

The party that cares less about the outcome of a negotiation is in the stronger negotiating position.

23

There is no stronger position at the negotiating table than indifference—to be able to walk away without negative consequence. This is not to say that a walk-away strategy is the best in every circumstance or over the long run; one can win many individual negotiating battles but lose a larger negotiating effort by alienating those with whom business could otherwise have been done in the future.

Win-win negotiating aims to satisfy both (or all) parties in a negotiation by employing meta-strategies: What is the next higher level of thinking that will give everyone what they want? Are the needs of the parties truly at odds with each other? Do the individual parties really know what is most important to them? Are they holding on to the things that are truly to their benefit, and willing to let go of the things that are not?

With regards to Professor Patrick Liles

24

There's a trolley every 15 minutes.

The opportunity in front of you may seem once-in-a-lifetime, but business opportunities are numerous. It is usually better to wait for or seek another opportunity than to rush into the present opportunity without performing due diligence—whether buying a car, house, or company. A "successful" entry into a bad business venture may be far worse than missing out entirely on a good business venture.

"You can always recover from the player you didn't sign. You may never recover from the player you signed at the wrong price."

—BILLY BEANE, General Manager of the Oakland A's,
quoted in *Moneyball* by Michael Lewis

Do your marketing while you're busy.

Opportunities can develop very slowly; it may be years from the time a new contact is made until it develops into business. If one waits until business slows down to initiate a marketing effort, it may be too late for it to help one get through the downturn.

Cannibalize your own sales.

27

Cannibalization is the diminishment of the sales of one's own product through the introduction of a competing product. But it is better to suffer a loss at one's own hands than to have a competitor introduce a product that takes away those same sales.

Putting an improved product on the market does not necessarily mean your older product must be discontinued. Because development, tooling, and other costs for the old product have been covered, the old product usually can be sold at a considerably lower price than the new product, giving customers the option of buying the old product at a low price or the new one at a higher price. It is important, however, that the new product offer something the older one does not in order to prevent confusion or resentment among customers.

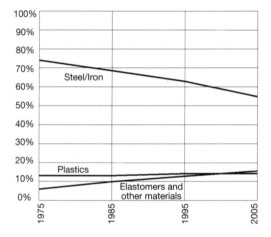

Automobile materials by weight

Source: Bayer Material Science AG

Substitutes are competitors.

28

When evaluating competitors, consider indirect competition as carefully as direct competition. Competition from substitutes can occur at many levels, including product, ingredient, service, and convenience. Plastic, for example, is a common product or ingredient substitute for, and thereby provides competition to, metal, glass, ceramics, and other materials. Online travel services are service substitutes for (and have largely eliminated) bricks-and-mortar travel agencies. Grocery stores that provide take-out food are convenience substitutes for traditional fast food restaurants. Even a clothesline is a substitute competitor to a clothes dryer.

Protections against product substitutes include strong brand identity, patents, and deliberately incompatible standards, such as the Apple versus PC computer operating systems.

Targeting the safe middle market is not necessarily a safe marketing strategy.

29

Consumers in the large middle market are often attracted to average quality products at decent prices. Targeting this market, particularly in the early years of a product's life, can be a viable strategy in many instances. But as a market matures, other factors compete with and take precedence over price for many consumers: styling, quality, features, and exclusivity. Brands that continue to target the middle of the market with a mid-priced product without giving a specific and compelling reason to buy it usually end up losing a lot of customers to niche competitors.

Free can be part of a successful business model.

30

Older businesses can be caught off-guard by the giveaway policies of newer businesses, for example newspapers that struggle to compete with online providers of free news content. But *free* has long been central to marketing: free admission before 7 p.m.; buy two get one free; children eat free when accompanied by (hungry, paying) adults.

Because free isn't really free, a giveaway must help a business sell its core item. Adobe gives away its Reader software but charges for its Acrobat program that makes screen readable documents. Google offers a free, stripped-down version of its SketchUp drawing program, which builds the skills and demand for its higher-powered for-sale version. Gevalia gives away coffee makers with the expectation that their new owners will fill them with the coffee Gevalia sells.

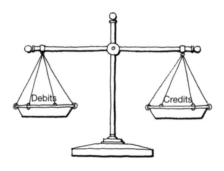

Double-entry bookkeeping

31

The record of a business's finances are maintained in a general ledger. A ledger shows the numerous accounts and sub-accounts in which the business records receipts and expenditures—Sales, Salaries, Utilities, Rent, and so on. "Double-entry" simply means that every transaction is recorded in two places, with the entry in one account offset by the entry in another. In this way, the books are always—except in the event of error—balanced.

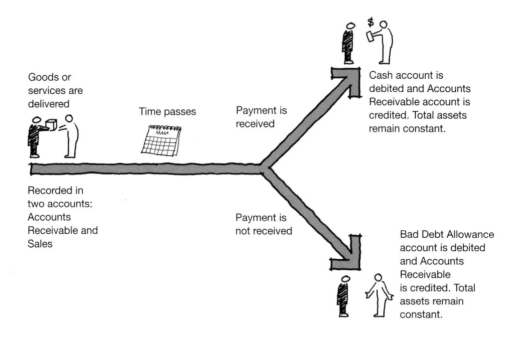

Goods or services are delivered

Recorded in two accounts: Accounts Receivable and Sales

Time passes

Payment is received

Cash account is debited and Accounts Receivable account is credited. Total assets remain constant.

Payment is not received

Bad Debt Allowance account is debited and Accounts Receivable is credited. Total assets remain constant.

Accrual accounting

Cash versus accrual accounting

32

Cash accounting shows income and expenses at the time cash is actually received or paid out. It works best in small organizations such as sole proprietorships.

Accrual accounting is more complex, but provides a more accurate snapshot of a company's status at any given time. It accommodates the frequent lag between when a purchase is made and cash changes hands. This requires that some accounting entries, such as bad debts, be estimated until final data becomes available. Most businesses use accrual accounting.

Liabilities

+ Owner's equity

= Assets

Balance sheet

Standard accounting reports

33

Balance Sheet: shows that what a company owns (assets) is equal to what it owes others (liabilities) plus the owners' equity (amounts invested by shareholders plus profits and losses kept within the company).

Income Statement (also called Profit and Loss or Earnings Statement): shows the performance of an organization over a period of time, such as one quarter or a year. The last line of the statement shows net profit or loss—hence the term "bottom line."

Statement of Cash Flows: shows where money came from and where it went.

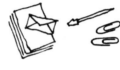

Depreciated

Not depreciated

Depreciation makes accounting more complex, but more accurate.

34

Depreciation is an accounting artifice that spreads the cost of long-term assets, such as buildings, vehicles, and equipment, over their expected useful lives. Without depreciation, an organization's financial picture can be distorted: The entire cost of a piece of equipment with a life expectancy of 25 years would be expensed in the year it was purchased, which could make the company appear highly unprofitable that year and inordinately profitable in subsequent years.

Straight-line depreciation allocates an equal share of cost to each year, while accelerated depreciation expenses a higher proportion of cost in the early years, when an asset may be more useful and maintenance costs are lower.

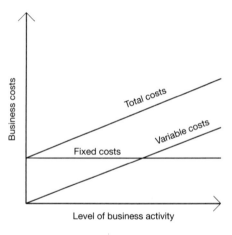

In the short term, some costs are fixed and some are variable. In the long run, all costs are variable.

35

Fixed costs are constant regardless of the level of business activity. For example, a hotel pays the same salary to a desk clerk whether one or ten guests register in an evening. Other fixed costs include depreciation, insurance, mortgage, and rent.

Variable costs depend on the level of business activity. For example, the cost of laundering linens depends on the number of occupied hotel rooms.

Fixed and variable costs both vary over longer periods of time. A permanent increase in the number of hotel guests might require the hiring of additional desk clerks, making staffing a variable cost in the long term. Also, the construction of additional hotel rooms may be called for, causing mortgage payments to increase to a new fixed level.

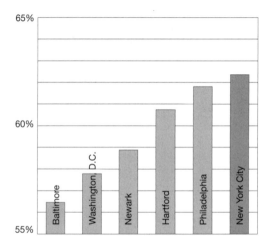

Landlord cost-to-income ratios

Financial ratios

Financial ratios reveal a company's performance over time (longitudinal analysis) or in comparison to competitors (cross-sectional analysis).

Leverage ratios measure the financial risk in an organization by comparing debt to equity or debt to assets. A lower proportion of debt indicates less risk, although a stable business with predictable revenues can safely have a higher leverage ratio.

36

Liquidity ratios compare short-term assets to short-term liabilities. A high ratio indicates a strong ability to meet obligations, but a very high ratio may indicate that assets are inefficiently allocated; e.g., some of the money on hand might be better used for investment.

Operating ratios measure efficiencies in day-to-day activities, e.g., the ratio of the cost of goods sold to sales, or net profit to gross profit.

Profitability ratios measure the ability to generate profits and include profit margin, return on assets, and return on net worth.

Solvency ratios measure the ability to meet long-term debt obligations by comparing short-term debt to total debt, and interest expense coverage.

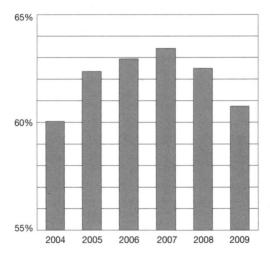

Landlord cost-to-income ratios

Use several accounting reports to gauge performance.

37

A financial statement for one period is useful, but static. An analysis of several consecutive reports can reveal trends and indicate if a business's overall condition is improving or deteriorating. Additionally, it is helpful to compare an organization's financial reports with those from other organizations in the same industry.

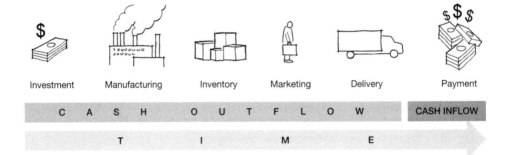

Investment · Manufacturing · Inventory · Marketing · Delivery · Payment

C A S H   O U T F L O W   CASH INFLOW

T I M E

Profitable, fast growing companies can be chronically short of cash.

38

A business typically makes a sale before payment is received from the buyer, while the costs related to that sale, such as materials, labor, commissions, and overhead, are borne up front. Consequently, a business that is profitable may be short of cash until payment is received. An especially fast growing company with rapidly increasing sales might be chronically short of cash.

Procuring and maintaining adequate capital is crucial for businesses. This can itself cost money, but the alternative is worse: Undercapitalization is among the most common causes of business failure; it can bring down an otherwise healthy organization.

Largest U.S. Bankruptcies, 1987–2008

Lehman Brothers	2008	$691,063,000,000
Worldcom	2002	103,914,000,000
Enron	2001	65,503,000,000
Conesco	2002	61,392,000,000
Pacific Gas and Electric	2001	36,152,000,000
Texaco	1987	34,940,000,000
Financial Corp. of America	1988	33,864,000,000
Refco	2005	33,333,000,000
IndyMac Bancorp	2008	32,734,000,000
Global Crossing Ltd.	2002	30,185,000,000
Bank of New England	1991	29,773,000,000
Calpine Corp.	2005	27,216,000,000

Source: New Generation Research, Inc.

Bankruptcy doesn't necessarily mean a business ceases to exist.

Chapter 7 bankruptcy is invoked when a business has inadequate assets, revenues, or markets to pay its debts and is unlikely to develop the ability to do so. It results in the dissolution of a business. Assets are sold off (liquidated) and the proceeds are used to pay overdue taxes, wages, and creditors. Any remaining cash is paid to stockholders.

39

Chapter 11 bankruptcy provides for the financial reorganization and continuation of a company that has insufficient cash to meet current debt obligations but healthy assets, markets, or other indicators suggesting likely profitability.

Most bankruptcies are voluntary; they are originated by the debtor. However, creditors may file a bankruptcy petition against a debtor. A company forced into Chapter 7 by its creditors may file under Chapter 11 to prevent its liquidation. Other forms of bankruptcy include Chapter 9 (municipal bankruptcy) and Chapter 13 (financial reorganization for individuals).

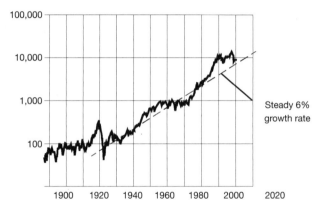

Dow Jones Industrial Average

The price of a stock is an emotional as well as economic projection.

Stock prices and stock market performance can fluctuate due to many factors, including macro-economic phenomena, interest rates, investor speculation, company performance, political events, and dividend payments. In theory, a stock's value derives from the value of the business that issues it. However, the selling price of a stock is whatever a willing buyer will pay a willing seller, and is based on the expectation each has for the company's future performance. Further, even the most accurate accounting of a company's performance contains guesswork—perhaps a hopeful estimate of returns not yet realized or a pessimistic approximation of debts from a failing venture—meaning that no economic value is established without some emotional component.

Although emotions cause volatility in individual stocks and the stock market in the short term, stock performance tends to be steady in the long run.

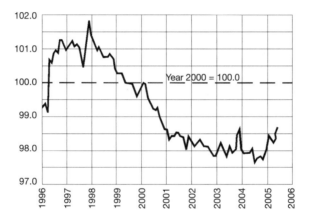

40

Japanese consumer price index

Deflation can be bad for business.

Inflation is a "normal" economic state: The value of money gradually decreases, leading to slowly rising prices and salaries. Modest inflation can help spur economic activity, as the threat of higher prices tomorrow may encourage the making of purchases and investments today.

Deflation may seem a positive occurrence because it increases the value of money. However, it can be dangerous for business when it occurs widely. In a deflationary environment, businesses and business customers may delay making ordinary investments and purchases in anticipation of better prices tomorrow and the next day. This can contribute to an economic slowdown, further depressing prices and stifling business activity. Additionally, falling prices usually mean falling profits, making it more difficult for a business to meet existing debt obligations.

When deflation occurs within a given industry or market segment due to a productivity increase, it is usually not problematic as profits are not adversely affected.

41

Monetary policy
U.S. Federal Reserve System

Fiscal policy
Executive and Legislative branches

The U.S. government has two primary tools for influencing the level of business activity.

Monetary policy is the province of the Federal Reserve System, the central banking system of the United States. The "Fed" has the ability to influence short-term interest rates and the money supply. Policies that reduce rates and/or increase the money supply make it less expensive for businesses to borrow and expand, but can increase inflation. The inverse is true as well.

Fiscal policy is the province of the Executive and Legislative branches. It refers to the rate, amount, and distribution of taxes and spending by the federal government. It takes longer to adjust than monetary policy.

42

One ad, one message.

Conveying too much information in one advertisement, no matter how accurate or positive, can confuse the audience and weaken the message. It's better to tell customers one thing likely to be important to them rather than everything that may be important about the product. Too, an ad campaign that features different information in different ads may reach more customers, as those who overlook one ad might respond positively to a different ad for the same product.

43

Repetition doesn't make a statement true, but it can make it believable.

44

Repetition can be an effective way of learning: It drills information into our memories. Even a false statement, repeated often enough, can be perceived as true. The *mere exposure effect* is why advertisements are often effective in changing beliefs and attitudes about products and brands, and is a major reason for repetition in advertising.

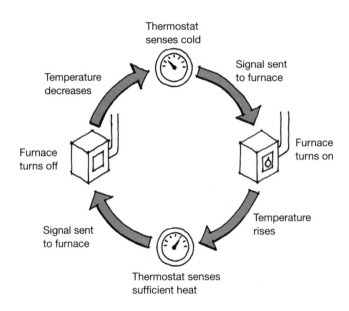

Thermostat
senses cold

Signal sent
to furnace

Furnace
turns on

Temperature
rises

Thermostat senses
sufficient heat

Signal sent
to furnace

Furnace
turns off

Temperature
decreases

A negative feedback loop

Positive and negative feedback loops

In a **negative feedback loop,** the system responds in the opposite direction of a stimulus, thereby providing overall stability or equilibrium. The Law of Supply and Demand usually functions as a negative feedback loop: When the supply of a product, material, or service increases, its price tends to fall, which may lead to rising demand, which will drive the price back up.

In a **positive feedback loop**, the system responds in the same direction as the stimulus, decreasing equilibrium further and further. For example, a consumer who feels prosperous after making new purchases may end up making even more purchases and take on excessive debt. Eventually, the consumer may face financial ruin and have to make a major correction by selling off assets or declaring bankruptcy. Because positive feedback loops restore equilibrium in their own, often dramatic way, it is sometimes suggested that positive feedback loops occur within a larger, if not directly visible, negative feedback loop.

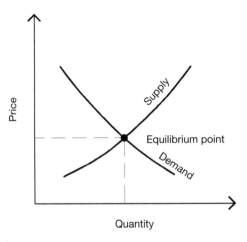

45

The Law of Supply and Demand doesn't always apply.

The Law of Supply and Demand says that if the supply of a given product or service exceeds demand, its price will decrease; if demand exceeds supply, its price will increase. Rising and falling prices impact demand similarly. When supply and demand are exactly equal, the market is at an equilibrium point and acts most efficiently: Suppliers sell all the goods they produce and consumers get all the goods they demand.

Not all products have historically adhered to the Law. When the prices of some luxury or prestige items have been lowered, demand has fallen due to reduced caché. In other instances, rising demand for a product has led to improvements in technology, increases in production efficiency, and the perfection of distribution channels, all of which have driven prices down. Electronic technologies have tended to follow this pattern.

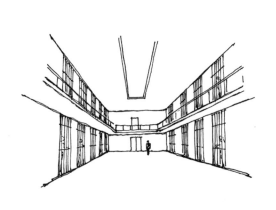

46

There never has been a true barter economy.

Despite common romanticizing of earlier societies in which money is imagined to have been unimportant or nonexistent, historians have found little evidence that any society has based its business enterprise primarily on barter. An exchange medium—minerals, spices, cash, or something else—has typically been used to attach value to items being exchanged. In prisons today, prisoners often buy from and sell items to each other using cigarettes as an exchange medium. When actual dollars become available on the yard, a twenty dollar bill might "sell" for several packs of cigarettes.

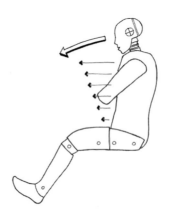

47

Those who say theory "isn't the real world" don't understand what theory is.

Theories explain real phenomena. They organize diverse bits of information into generalizing patterns, identify underlying reasons for why things happen as they do, suggest the deeper nature of the things we know and those we do not quite know, help transfer knowledge from one enterprise to another, and suggest the likely outcomes of new situations.

Businesspeople averse to theory may thrive in business as long as the parameters familiar to them remain in place. Those who embrace theory are more likely to adapt to, and even seek out, new beneficial situations.

48

"There's nothing so practical as a good theory."

—KURT LEWIN (1890–1947)

49

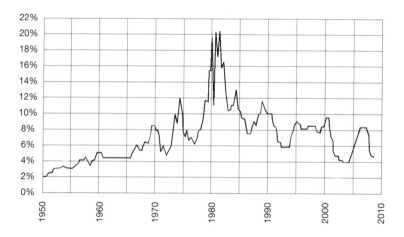

Average U.S. prime rate

Interest rates have three components.

The **real rate of interest** is the compensation a lender theoretically would require to make a risk-free loan in an inflation-free environment. It serves to compensate the lender for postponing his or her own use of the money.

An **inflation premium** is added to the real rate of interest so that the principal (the original amount of the loan), once repaid, has the same purchasing power as when the loan was originated.

A **risk premium** is added to compensate the lender for assuming the risk that the principal will not be repaid.

Additionally, lenders may require borrowers to pay *points* in order to cover administrative costs or to procure a lower interest rate.

Annual Percentage Rate (APR) ▷	1%	2%	3%	4%	5%	6%	7%	8%	9%
Approx. years to double investment ▷	72	36	24	18	14.2	12	10.3	9	8

The Rule of 72

The Rule of 72 estimates the number of years needed to double an investment when the interest rate is known: Simply divide 72 by the interest rate. An investment returning 9% interest per year will double in approximately eight (72 ÷ 9) years. Greater accuracy may be achieved by using 69 or 70, but 72 is usually more convenient as it has more divisors.

51

The formula can be reversed to calculate an interest rate when the time of return is known, or to calculate the halving of monetary value due to inflation. For example, at 4% annual inflation, one dollar will have half the buying power in 18 years (72 ÷ 4).

A business buys a copy machine because it needs copies, not because it wants a copy machine.

Customers make purchases to solve problems. A good salesperson first seeks to understand the true nature and extent of a customer's problem, and only then offers a solution. Often, the solution is very different from the one the customer assumed. A good salesperson will even talk a customer out of making a wrong purchase, because in the long run the customer will respect the salesperson's honesty and may become a repeat customer.

52

Customers do not buy a product or service the same way or for the same reason.

Consumers are organized by marketers into segments distinguished by age, geography, interests, income, and similar factors. A different marketing mix of the **Four P's** is used to reach each segment.

Product: an offering's features, style, variety (e.g., cane sugar, granulated sugar, light brown sugar, etc.), packaging (single-serving packets, five-pound packages, etc.), and brand name.

Price: the list price, discounts, allowances, and payment terms.

Promotion: advertising, personal selling, sales promotions, and public relations. A product aimed at young buyers, for example, might emphasize web-based promotion over print advertising.

Place: the venue for purchase and the logistics of moving products from manufacturer to consumer; for example, whether the product will be sold through authorized retailers only, in vending machines, etc.

Some experts refer to the **Five P's** (including packaging), or the **Six P's** (people).

53

Feature

Benefit

A feature is a fact. A benefit is how it helps the customer.

Pointing out the features of a product to customers does not mean they will understand why the features are useful; one has to explain their direct benefit. For example, call forwarding and call waiting are features; never missing another call is their benefit. Benefits, not features, ultimately sell products.

54

Complaints can be good things.

When a customer tells a business where it failed, he or she is doing the business a favor. For every unsatisfied customer who complains, many others quietly leave and never come back. A complaining customer usually wants to continue doing business with the company—he or she just wants something to change so the relationship can continue. In fact, customers whose complaints are resolved quickly and satisfactorily often become very loyal: They make larger purchases, become personally attached to the business and its employees, and provide positive word-of-mouth.

There are costs to keeping customers satisfied, but the cost of recruiting new customers is higher. In fact, a satisfied customer may even pay more for the product or service.

55

"Your most unhappy customers are your greatest source of learning."

—BILL GATES, *Business @ the Speed of Thought*

56

Branding

A good brand is not only recognizable; it has real meaning to consumers—perhaps reliability, safety, cutting-edge styling, lifestyle identity, or environmental sustainability.

A **brand extension** is the introduction of a known brand into a new product category, such as when a clothing designer begins offering a line of shoes. Brand familiarity can lead to faster acceptance of a new product. However, if the new product is too different from existing products sold under the same name—for example, motorcycle manufacturer Harley Davidson's introduction of a wine cooler in the 1970s—confusion can result in the marketplace, and the overall brand image may be at least temporarily tarnished.

57

Frederick de Moleyns of Great Britain received
the first patent for an incandescent lamp in 1841.

Intellectual property protection

The United States Constitution grants Congress the power "to promote the progress of science and useful arts, by securing for limited times to authors and inventors the exclusive right to their respective writings and discoveries." In the U.S., the following protections are available:

Trademark: a distinctive word, phrase, image, sound, fragrance, or combination used by an individual or business to distinguish its goods. Registration with the U.S. Patent and Trademark Office results in formal legal ownership, although registration is not always necessary to establish ownership. An unregistered trademark may be indicated by ™, while a registered mark is indicated by ®. ℠ may be used to indicate a mark for services.

Patent: a protection granted by the USPTO giving an inventor the right to exclude others from making, using, offering for sale, or importing the same invention. Patents usually last for 20 years from the date of filing.

Copyright: applies to expressions of ideas, including literary, musical, dramatic, pictorial, artistic, and architectural works; motion pictures, musical compositions, sound recordings, software, and radio and television broadcasts. A copyright registered with the U.S. Copyright Office generally endures for the life of the creator plus 70 years.

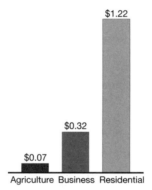

58

$1.22

$0.32

$0.07

Agriculture Business Residential

Amount spent by municipalities on services (water, sewer, roads, police, etc.) for every $1.00 received in tax revenue

Source: The Garreau Group

Business development can save municipalities money.

Although considered undesirable in some bedroom communities, business development is more cost effective for municipalities than a comparable level of residential development. Businesses typically pay higher real estate taxes than residents do, while demanding far less in services.

59

Materials are "free"; it's everything else that costs money.

All business costs can be very generally categorized as either material costs or human costs. However, material costs have human costs embedded in them. For example, the cost of a material purchased at retail has embedded in it the costs of all previous labor, profit, licenses, transportation, tariffs, etc., that helped bring it to the point of sale. When a product is traced back to its origin—as a raw material in the ground—material costs ultimately vanish.

60

Producers

Intermediaries
- promote and advertise products
- match quantities to market needs
- negotiate prices and terms
- store, finance, and transport inventories
- assume risks of theft, damage, and obsolescence

Consumers

Are retailers and wholesalers necessary?

Wouldn't it be better for everyone if products were sold directly by producers to consumers, bypassing the markups of intermediaries such as distributors, wholesalers, and retailers?

In actual practice, no. If intermediaries did not exist, manufacturers would have to assume their duties, greatly increasing their costs and operational complexity. If chewing gum, for example, were not sold through intermediaries, a manufacturer would have to sell gum to each person who wanted it—an impossible task!

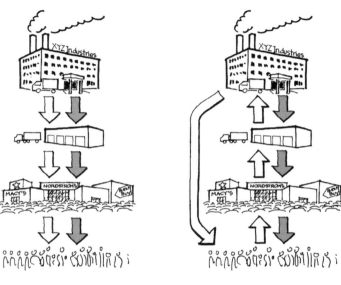

61

Push strategy   Pull strategy

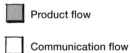

Product flow

Communication flow

Push and pull

In **push strategies**, manufacturers promote their product to intermediaries by offering, for example, free in-store promotional displays and price discounts, in an effort to get them to carry and promote their product to consumers. Push strategies are most effective when an item is an impulse purchase, brand loyalty is low, or when consumers already understand a product's benefits.

In **pull strategies**, the manufacturer promotes the product directly to consumers, perhaps by providing coupons and free samples, to encourage them to request the item from retailers. This strategy works best when brand loyalty is high and there are perceived differences between brands.

62

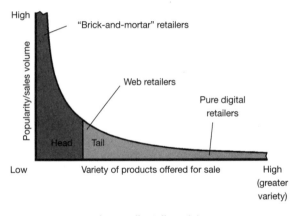

High

"Brick-and-mortar" retailers

Popularity/sales volume

Web retailers

Pure digital
retailers

Head | Tail

Low

Variety of products offered for sale

High
(greater
variety)

Long tail retail model

With regards to Chris Anderson

The Internet encourages a long tail business model.

Traditional retail stores have limited and rather expensive floor space, and thus stock a comparatively narrow range of items that they sell in large amounts to a local, relatively small customer base. In a long tail model, a business does the opposite: It sells a very wide range of items, each in comparatively small amounts, to a large customer base, often over a very wide geographic area. Online retailers often take a long tail approach because they can be located in low-traffic, inexpensive areas where it is affordable to warehouse slow-moving items.

Digital retailers—those selling purely digital products over the web—require effectively no warehouse space, allowing them to stock obscure, extremely low-selling items with almost no inventory cost.

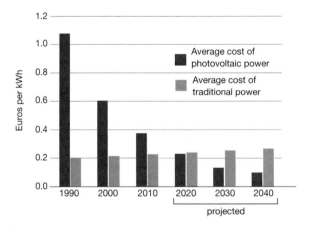

63

Costs in Europe for photovoltaic (solar) energy
versus traditional energy

Source: Winifred Hoffman via Travis Bradford,
Solar Revolution (MIT Press, 2006)

Going green can make more "green."

Environmentally sensitive business practices have traditionally been engaged more for ecological concern than economic benefit. But in the longer run, after the initial capital costs of alternative energy infrastructure are recouped, a greater return on investment can often be realized. For example, it will initially cost a business more to install a geothermal energy system than a conventional heating system. But once paid for, geothermal energy is effectively free. In fact, the gap in cost between traditional and alternative energies continually narrows, indicating a convergence in the near future.

64

An expert isn't always the person who knows the most.

Experts are expected to know a lot, but often it is better to know how to organize and structure knowledge than to simply *have* knowledge. Innovative thinkers don't merely retain and recite information; they identify and create new patterns that reorganize known information.

65

True experts know more than they know they know.

You are riding a bicycle and it begins to fall to the left…which way should you turn the handlebars to stay balanced?

Surveys show that most people will answer "to the right," but the correct answer is "to the left." And interestingly, when riding a bicycle, nearly everyone will correctly and intuitively turn the handlebars to the left.

This discrepancy exists because our unconscious, intuitive mind is aware of things our conscious mind is not. Often, one has to be *in action* in order to know the right thing to do. Effective businesspeople must make decisions on the fly, and must learn when to trust—and mistrust—their rational and intuitive capacities for judgment.

66

Promoting the best performer to manager is often a mistake.

Employees who excel in one area of business are often promoted to supervisory positions. But in management, one's achievements are measured through the actions of others. A first-rate lab researcher promoted to lab supervisor, for example, has to coach, mentor, manage, and help other researchers make discoveries—something that may be beyond his or her abilities or interests. Compounding the problem for the organization is that the department no longer has its best researcher making discoveries on the bench.

Management is its own area of expertise, distinct in many ways from the activity being managed. In large organizations in business and government, top-level managers often lack expertise in the work being done, but are able to create circumstances in which those under them may thrive.

67

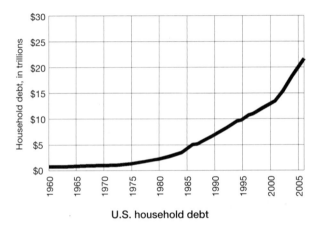

U.S. household debt

Source: U.S. Federal Reserve Bank

Why buy debt?

"Purchasing debt" is a bit of a misnomer: When one buys debt he or she does not actually end up with more debt. Rather, he or she acquires the right to collect money previously owed to the selling party. Debts owed by private citizens and businesses to banks, finance agencies, utility companies, medical care providers, and other businesses can sometimes be purchased for pennies on the dollar. The lower the likelihood of collecting the debt, the lower its price.

68

The higher one rises in an organization, the longer it takes to implement a decision.

Front-line managers can effect immediate changes by directly instructing workers. A sales manager can redirect the activities of salespeople immediately, and an accounting manager can make immediate changes in bookkeeping practices.

At higher levels of an organization, where employees are more concerned with strategic matters, decisions take more time to implement. If the vice president of marketing wishes to change the style of a product being produced, considerable time will be required to engage feasibility studies, explore design alternatives, investigate the technical methods required, and alter manufacturing methods.

69

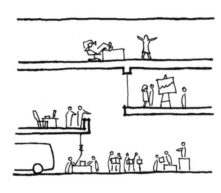

The higher one rises in an organization, the more one must be a generalist.

At the lower levels of an organization, employees usually have direct knowledge of specific activities. Production employees, for example, know how to handle materials, assemble products, test performance, and troubleshoot very specific problems. However, they may know little about other activities of the company.

A manager often lacks such specific knowledge but has generalized understandings of personnel, training, motivation techniques, evaluation, product distribution, compensation, and budgeting. A vice president will be engaged in still broader activities across more areas of the company, including long range planning, product development, financing, and strategic direction. At the highest executive levels, officers and board members may be concerned with the philosophical direction of the company, the organization's mission, and the meanings of the company's brand in the market.

70

Guy Kawasaki's Favorite Books

The Innovator's Dilemma
by Clayton M. Christensen
The Effective Executive
by Peter F. Drucker
Crossing the Chasm
by Geoffrey A. Moore
The Hockey Handbook
by Lloyd Percival
Uncommon Genius
by Denise Shekerjian
If You Want to Write
by Brenda Ueland
Mastering the Dynamics of Innovation
by James M. Utterback

Bill Gates's Favorite Books

The Blind Watchmaker
by Richard Dawkins
The Catcher in the Rye
by J. D. Salinger
My Years with General Motors
by Alfred P. Sloan
The Great Gatsby
by F. Scott Fitzgerald
The Language Instinct
by Steven Pinker

Sources: GuyKawasaki.com; Pinellas Park Public Library, Pinellas Park, FL

"If you want to be a leader, you've got to be a reader."

—DR. DAVID NOEBEL

71

Good, fast, or cheap: pick two.

The geometry of a triangle is such that its sides are interdependent; one cannot alter one side without affecting the rest of the triangle. The Quality-Time-Cost Triangle suggests that if one wants high quality work (side one) performed quickly (a second side), she will have to cede control of the third side and pay a higher price. If she wants work done quickly at a low price, the quality of the work is likely to be lower. If she wants high quality work performed inexpensively, time will have to be sacrificed, because she will have to spend considerable time searching for the lowest possible bidder, and is likely to wait longer for the low bidder to perform the work at his or her pace and convenience.

Variations on the triangle include Quality-Price-Service (a given product sold at a lower price will likely be accompanied by poorer customer service) and Quality-Time-Control (to get a high quality project completed quickly, one will have to yield control of most of the decision making to the person doing the work).

72

If all courses of action appear equal, get more objective information.

When feeling stuck while weighing an important decision, it is almost always helpful to seek out new, objective information on any aspect of the matter—even if
the effort or information to be gained initially seems of little value. Even the most
modest new data on a market, client, or technology, when probed seriously, can
provoke expansive new insights that point toward a more informed decision.

73

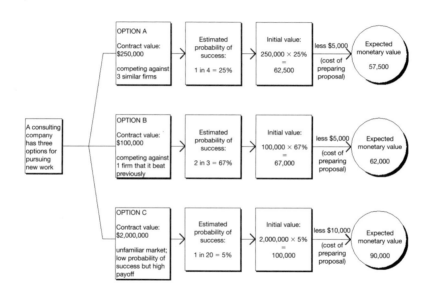

The decision tree

A decision tree compares the likely outcomes of various courses of action. Estimates of the probability and value of each alternative are established and the results are compared.

Decision trees help temper subjective considerations and guesswork, and guard against decision making that is randomized, hunch-based, or emotional. For example, a businessperson who once failed in pursuing a particular market or client might fear pursuing that market or client again; a decision tree can help show if such fears are reasonable.

Decision trees cannot entirely objectify decision making unless the variables are entirely mechanical, rational, or quantified. They are also of limited use when the options they map have wide divergencies in probability or value. For example, a 100% chance of receiving $1,000 would be for many a superior option to a 1% chance of $100,000 payoff, even though mathematically equal.

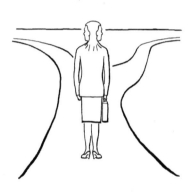

74

A good manager makes imperfect decisions.

It is rare for circumstances to permit the collection of ideal data to support a pending decision. The time, effort, and expense required to do so must be weighed against the potential benefit as well as the dangers of delay. A good manager knows:

- when to make a good or workable decision and when to attempt a perfect decision
- when to live with and when to correct a previous bad decision
- that no decision or a belated decision is often worse than a bad decision
- that the right decision is sometimes the one made right in follow-up
- that even the best decision makers make mistakes, and that a manager is properly judged on a long-term record.

75

"Not to decide is to decide."

—HARVEY COX

76

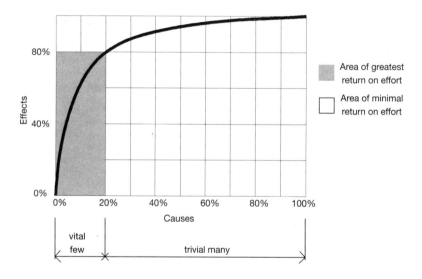

The Pareto Principle

Sacrifice the trivial few for the vital many.

The **Pareto Principle,** a concept created by Joseph Juran, says that 20% of causes are usually responsible for 80% of results. This suggests that businesses are best served by giving the most attention to the 20% of customers accounting for 80% of its sales, to the 20% of the effort that will do 80% of the work, or to solving the 20% of factors causing 80% of its problems. Some will even argue that 80% of the work in an organization is done by 20% of its people.

77

Two views on good management

Good managers delegate. A manager is responsible to the big picture, and lets those under him or her handle the details and overflow.

Good managers serve those under them. A manager exists to expedite the work of staff, and does whatever is required to help those under him or her do the "real" work.

78

Tell others the result you need, not how to get it.

Micromanagement does not always mean overmanaging the little things, but more often the "middle" things. A good manager thus acts at two extremes of scale—

- **the most general values** to guide an endeavor. For example, honor functionality over aesthetics, achieve community consensus, and make sure the product is fun to use.
- **the most specific details** to be achieved in the outcome. For example, the product must weigh less than 13 ounces, it can't be orange, the power switch has to be on the right, and all design work must be completed within exactly three months.

—and leaves it to workers to engage the middle ground as they see fit. Telling others exactly how to do their work takes away their initiative, but giving them freedom to shape their own work allows them to become creative and to grow personally invested in the endeavor.

As progress warrants, a manager should seek to remind the team of the general values and specific details, and help the team redefine them.

79

When overwhelmed, try doing fewer things, but doing them better.

Business owners, managers, employees, and students can become overwhelmed, distracted, and frustrated by trying to do too many things perfectly. When having difficulty maintaining quality standards, achieving desired outcomes, meeting schedule and cost targets, or getting others to prioritize and perform well, see if you can't reduce the number of things being attempted, and focus on doing them better.

There are important tasks that must be done promptly, unimportant tasks that must be done promptly, important tasks with no particular rush, and unimportant tasks with no particular rush; and sometimes there are things that seem crucial but may not need doing at all.

80

Obsolete does not always mean useless.

There are two types of obsolescence. **Functional obsolescence** means a device can no longer perform its intended function or cannot perform it efficiently or safely, and should be replaced. **Technological obsolescence** means that newer technologies have replaced the old, although the original device may still perform reliably, quickly, and safely.

Although having the latest and best is appealing, it is sometimes, or even often, better to push old technology to its limits than to feel obligated to invest in the new.

81

Form, storm, norm, perform.

Group facilitation helps groups with diverse interests forge common goals. Professional facilitators usually know little about the fields in which they consult, but are expert in helping others forge a common direction. They are neutral; they lead discussion and debate but not outcomes. One popular sequence of facilitation is:

Form: Organize the event; discuss the agenda; set expectations and ground rules; establish a schedule; outline the problem and the desired goals.

Storm (brainstorm): Solicit as many strategies and solutions as possible from all participants. Do not critique; record even those options that appear unlikely.

Norm: Discuss implications of the storming alternatives; identify common patterns and areas of overlap; categorize by similarity; identify hierarchies.

Perform: Help the group agree on a solution or course of action; determine what needs to be done next.

82

Facilitation is never a pure, linear process; iterations or fractals of the F-S-N-P cycle are typically found within each phase. Moreover, groups often find that upon proceeding to Performing, they regress and must reengage the process at an earlier stage.

Risk homeostasis

Risk homeostasis theory says that people have an innate sense of the level of risk they consider acceptable; when a given system is made safer, they behave more recklessly and at least partially nullify the safety gains.

A study at the University of Bath found that drivers drove measurably closer to bicyclists who were wearing helmets than those not wearing helmets. Taxicab drivers in Munich driving vehicles with anti-lock brakes took corners faster and left shorter reaction zones than drivers of cabs with conventional brakes; the two groups ultimately had the same crash rate.

83

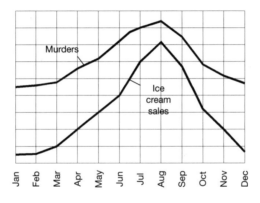

A statistical correlation does not necessarily mean a cause-effect relationship.

Begun in 1924, the Hawthorne Studies, conducted at Western Electric Company, found that employees worked more efficiently under altered lighting conditions. It was initially concluded that the lighting caused the improvement in production. Years later, it was realized that workers worked better not necessarily because of the lighting, but because they knew they were being intensively observed.

84

Moral hazard

When organizations and individuals are not required to bear the negative conse-
quences of their failures, a moral hazard exists. A lender insured by the government against loan default, for example, may make very risky, high interest loans to
uncreditworthy customers because the lender will do no worse than break even,
and at best will realize a very high rate of return.

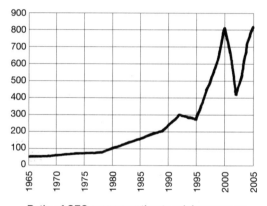

Ratio of CEO compensation to minimum wage

Source: Economic Policy Institute

"The ideal from the point of view of the employer is to have output without employees, and the ideal from the point of view of the employee is to have income without employment."

—E. F. SCHUMACHER (1911–1977),
Small Is Beautiful

86

Darker backgrounds are usually better when images, such as photos of products, are more important.

Lighter backgrounds are usually better for web pages in which text is more important.

Don't leave the design of your website to the IT department.

A successful website requires a high level of technical execution, including the coordination of information and links, writing of HTML code, manipulation of video and still images, and the updating of content. Information Technology experts are crucial to this process, but the essence of a good website is found among a different set of concerns—the company's brand identity, the nature of the other media in which the company reaches customers, and the logical-intuitive complexities of customer interface—that transcends the execution of technical tasks.

87

Microenterprise

Large, multinational businesses have capabilities that small, local businesses do not, but small businesses also perform important economic functions. Studies have shown that money spent in a locally owned business has two to four times the impact on the local economy than the same amount spent at a corporate chain.

The majority of businesses in the United States are small, local businesses. In fact, every business was, at some point in its lineage, a small business. Without small businesses, there would be no big businesses.

88

"All people are entrepreneurs, but many don't have the opportunity to find that out."

—MUHAMMAD YUNUS,
Founder of the Grameen Bank

89

In retail, know if your business is a host or a parasite.

Retail shop owners usually expect their establishments to draw many visitors. But the vast majority of retail stores are not destinations; customers do not travel specifically to them. Rather, these businesses must rely on other, often larger businesses nearby to generate sufficient traffic.

Businesses and other entities that inherently draw a lot of visitors are often called anchors. Locating a small business near an anchor is an excellent way to increase foot traffic, and between two anchors is even better. For example, a newsstand, dry-cleaning establishment, or coffee shop sited modestly between a car park and commuter ferry may be in a better location than one with its own "destination" parking lot, because of the morning and evening foot traffic between the two anchors. Similarly, a sandwich shop located midway between a trade school and public transit station may get much more traffic than one located very close to one anchor but in the opposite direction from the other anchor.

90

Good merchandising is theater.

Consumers buy products at retail because they want or need them. But that may not be why they walk through the front door of a store; and without a compelling reason to visit a store many people will shop online.

What can your retail business offer that will make the experience of your store as interesting as or more interesting than the items you sell? What aspect of performance—product demonstrations, kinetic rather than static physical displays, even store pets—can be the "accidental" reason customers visit your store and buy from you?

Highest Profit Margins by Industry

Industry	Net Profit Margin
REIT,* Healthcare Facilities	36.00%
Application Software	22.60%
Publishing–Periodicals	18.60%
Cigarettes	18.30%
Agricultural Chemicals	17.70%
REIT,* Residential	17.30%
Networking & Communication Devices	16.80%
Drug Manufacturers–Major	16.50%
Beverages–Brewers	16.00%
Industrial Metals & Minerals	15.80%

*Real Estate Investment Trust

Source: Yahoo Finance

Set prices according to what the customer will pay, not necessarily according to costs.

Customers are unlikely to know a business's costs or profitability on a given item. A business therefore shouldn't restrict its markup to what it thinks customers will deem reasonable. It's vital to know the costs of bringing a product or service to the customer and also the competition's pricing, but best to set a price based on the customers' perception of value.

92

An effective speaker knows his or her subject, but first seeks to know the audience.

Three key questions help focus preparation for a presentation:

1. What does the audience already know? The answer will tell you where to begin your presentation. By beginning with a recap of shared knowledge or interests, the audience will feel grounded and will be more receptive to receiving new knowledge or an alternate point of view.

2. What is at stake? A speaker can easily assume that matters of importance to him or her are of evident importance to the audience. But audiences usually need to be shown what is at stake for them. A presentation is all the more effective if the audience's stakes are shared with those of the speaker.

3. What does the audience need to learn? Do you want to give the audience the next incremental step in its learning? Or do you wish to give a leapfrog presentation that goes far beyond their current knowledge, motivating the audience to do "fill-in" work? And among all you wish to impart, what is the one crucial takeaway?

The real purpose of a visual presentation is to get people to *listen*, not look.

It can be tempting to pack slides or presentation boards with extra information to look smart or give the audience extra value. But the most effective visual presentations are clear, concise, and even terse. Limit text on visual props to a few titles, subtitles, phrases, and talking points—five or six is usually the maximum. Save your best material for the words you speak.

94

Write it once.

A well-written contract defines or explains each term or condition only once. Subsequent mentions of that term or condition refer to, or are presumed to refer to, the original explanation. Repeating contract language in an effort to impart greater emphasis is dangerous, as differences in context can lead to confusion in meaning and an unfavorable interpretation in a court of law. Further, because negotiations invariably require the editing of contract language, a redundantly drafted contract will require changes in multiple locations—leading to the possibility that one location will be missed and an inconsistent document will result.

Say it twice.

Regardless of how clear we are in verbal communications, misunderstandings occur. To minimize miscommunications, end every conversation or meeting with a summary of conclusions, including the participants' responsibilities and next steps. Saying things a bit differently the second time often helps uncover misunderstandings.

When assigning a new task, ask the assignee to demonstrate in writing, if only a brief e-mail, his or her understanding of it. This will give both parties an opportunity to correct any misunderstandings before they impair performance.

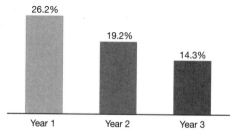

26.2%

19.2%

14.3%

Year 1   Year 2   Year 3

Restaurant failures by year of operation

Source: "Why Restaurants Fail," Cornell University, 2005

Running a restaurant well is about more than being a good chef.

Many small businesses fail because their owners mistake their passion for a field for the desire to run a business in that field. But successful business owners know that the *business* of business—marketing, financing, hiring, training, firing, planning, negotiating, purchasing, balancing the books, maintaining the physical plant, resolving employee tiffs, and much more—must receive primary attention if their passion is to have a safe haven.

Love your passion, but *know* your business.

97

Anything Company
- Pete's records
  - Current stuff
  - Miscellaneous stuff
  - Old stuff
  - Other misc. stuff
- Finance
  - Loans
  - Payroll
  - Money
  - Void stuff
- New jobs
  - Advertising
  - Jill's accounts
  - Customer service
- Important office info
- Personnel
  - Bill
  - Mary
  - Todd
- Production
  - Alice's records
  - Manufacturing

Confusing

Anything Company
- Administration
- Finance
  - Accounts Payable
  - Accounts Receivable
  - Financial Statements
  - Inventory
  - Payroll
- Human Resources
  - Office Personnel
  - Production Personnel
  - Sales Personnel
- Marketing
  - Advertising
  - Current Leads
  - Customer Service
- Physical plant
  - Building
  - Equipment
  - Utilities
- Production
  - Manufacturing
  - Vendors

Better

Even a one-person business has departments.

All businesses have similar concerns and responsibilities, including marketing, research, development, purchasing, production, management, accounting, human resources, and customer service. In a large business, a department may have hundreds or thousands of employees; in a sole proprietorship a department may consist of a folder on a hard drive and a few hours of work per month by the proprietor.

Accepting the universality of departments is essential to setting up and growing a business, as it encourages the employment of standards and practices that others can readily understand. Even arranging and naming computer folders and files by a more universal, rather than idiosyncratic, standard can help future growth occur more naturally.

98

Hire your boss.

When a sole proprietor adds staff for the first time, a clear decision must be made as to whether the new employee:

- will work **under the proprietor**;
- will be an approximate **peer to the proprietor**; or
- will have some **authority over the proprietor**.

The last option is best for many small-businesspeople. For example, a home-based web designer who hires two employees to meet a growing workload might quickly become preoccupied with scheduling, billing, payroll, troubleshooting, and supervising, and be disappointed to be doing very little of the design work she loves. In such situations, it is often best to hire someone to manage the "business of the business" in order to remain focused on the things one most enjoys.

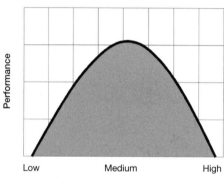

Some stress is good. A lot of stress is bad.

Stress has many causes: tight deadlines, financial constraints, demanding customers, aggressive competition, and the expectations of work colleagues. The Yerkes-Dodson Law says that performance increases with stress, but only up to a point. When arousal due to stress is too high, performance decreases.

Studies have also shown that performance response can initially decrease under stress, and increase as the body and/or mind cope with the stressor. But one can endure stress for only so long before performance declines and exhaustion is reached.

100

"We survive by breathing but we can't say we live to breathe. Likewise, making money is very important for a business to survive, but money alone cannot be the reason for business to exist."

—ANU AGA,
Former Chair, Thermax Ltd.

Michael W. Preis is a visiting professor of business administration at the University of Illinois at Urbana-Champaign. After graduating from the Harvard Business School he worked as a management consultant, executive, and business owner before earning a PhD in marketing from George Washington University.

Matthew Frederick is an architect, urban designer, teacher, author of the bestselling *101 Things I Learned in Architecture School*, and the creator, editor, and illustrator of the 101 Things I Learned series. He lives in Cambridge, Massachusetts.